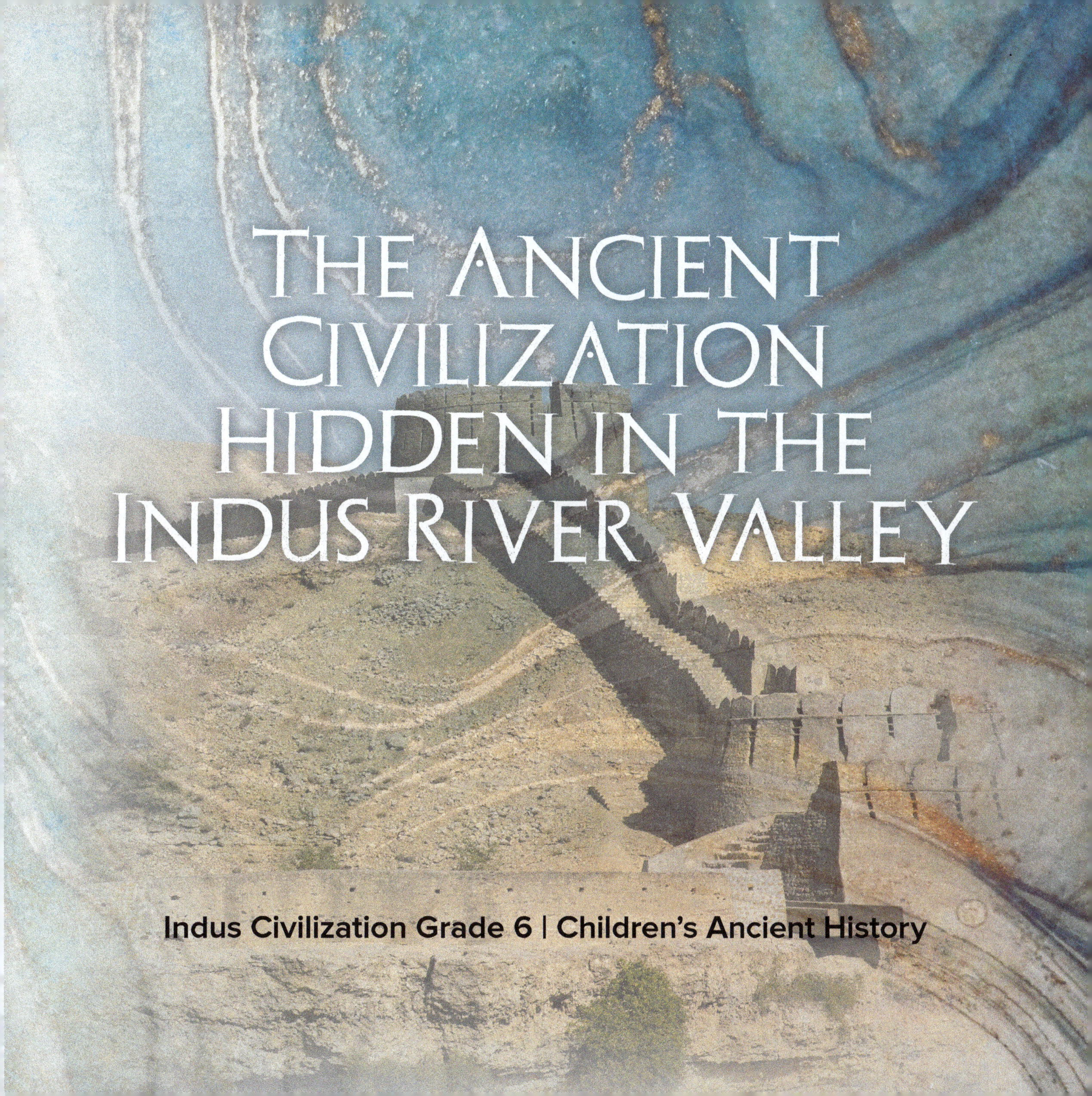

The Ancient Civilization Hidden in the Indus River Valley

Indus Civilization Grade 6 | Children's Ancient History

BABY PROFESSOR
EDUCATION KIDS

First Edition, 2021

Published in the United States by Speedy Publishing LLC, 40 E Main Street, Newark, Delaware 19711 USA.

10 9 8 7 6 * 5 4 3 2 1

Print Edition: 9781541954687
Digital Edition: 9781541957688
Hardcover Edition: 9781541983694

See the world in pictures. Build your knowledge in style.
www.speedypublishing.com

Table of Contents

Indus River Valley, Himalayas, Ladakh, India

The ruins of the ancient civilization of the Indus River Valley in India lay hidden beneath the earth for centuries until the end of the 19th century. That's when workers happened upon some unusual artifacts. As archaeologists began excavating, they discovered the remains of a flourishing civilization that thrived in the region from about 2500 to 1500 BC.

Archaeologists theorize that the ancient civilization sprang up at this location because of the bounty of the Indus River, but that it fell due to an invasion from the East. Let's examine the hidden ancient civilization of the Indus River Valley, its rise, and its fall.

A patchwork of corn and barley fields in the Indus River Valley as seen from Thiksey Monastery in Ladakh, India.

Where Is the Indus River?

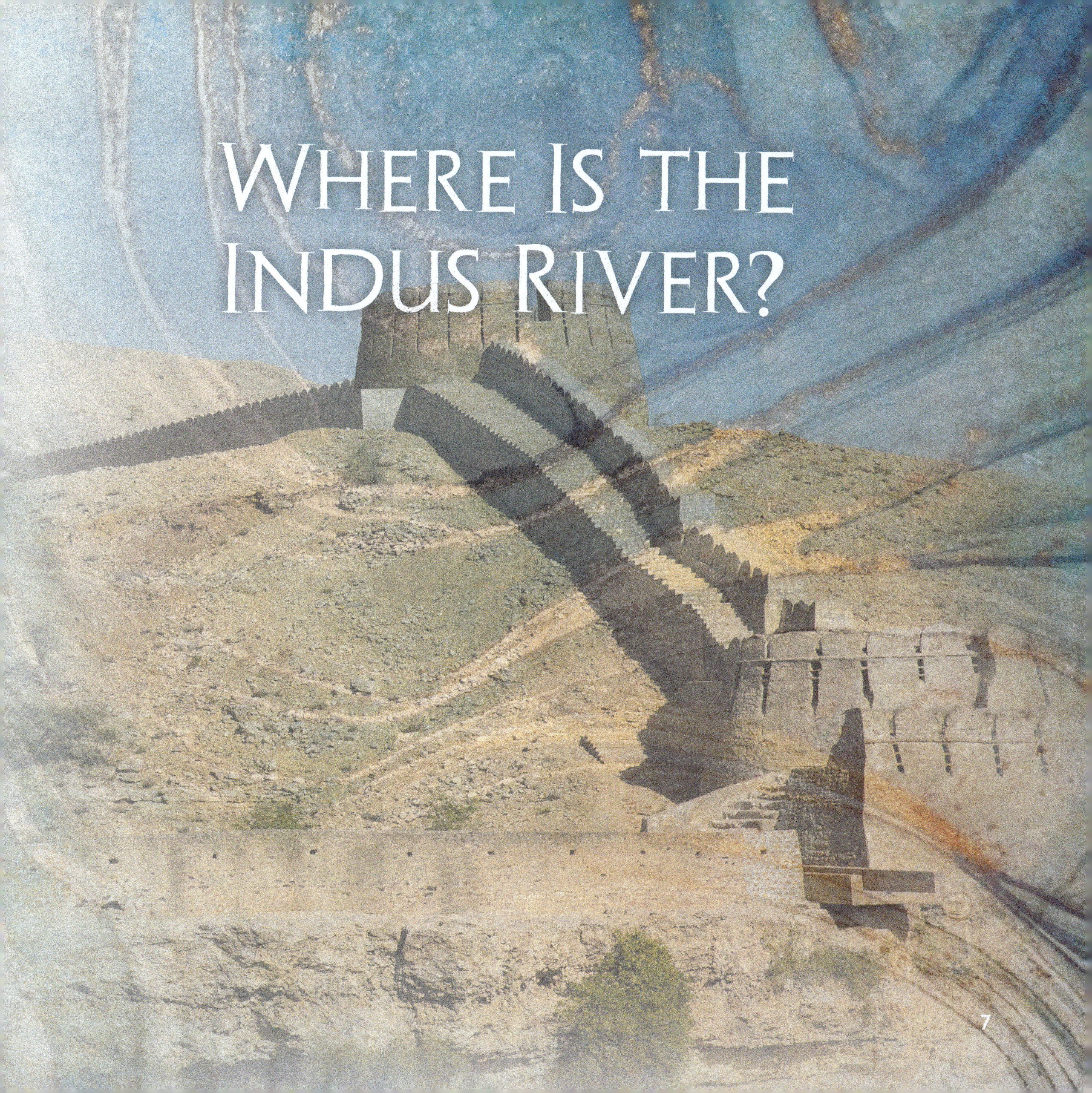

The Indus River begins in the Himalayan Mountains. It flows through what is now India and into the northern part of Pakistan before emptying into the Arabian Sea at the southern end of Pakistan.

The Indus River flows through India and into the northern part of Pakistan before emptying into the Arabian Sea at the southern end of Pakistan.

Sharp curve of Indus river, rocky mountain range and wide area of sand in Skardu, Gilgit Balistan, Pakistan.

The Indus River forms a valley. On one side of the valley is a desert region. There are tall mountains on the other sides.

The Indus River deposits rich nutrients along its banks making the soil fertile and ideal for farming.

Along its 2,000-mile journey, the powerful river deposits rich nutrients along its banks. This makes the soil fertile and ideal for farming. This region is prone to heavy monsoons that swell rivers to flood their banks. The seasonal flooding was beneficial for replenishing the soil.

The Significance of the Indus River Valley's Location

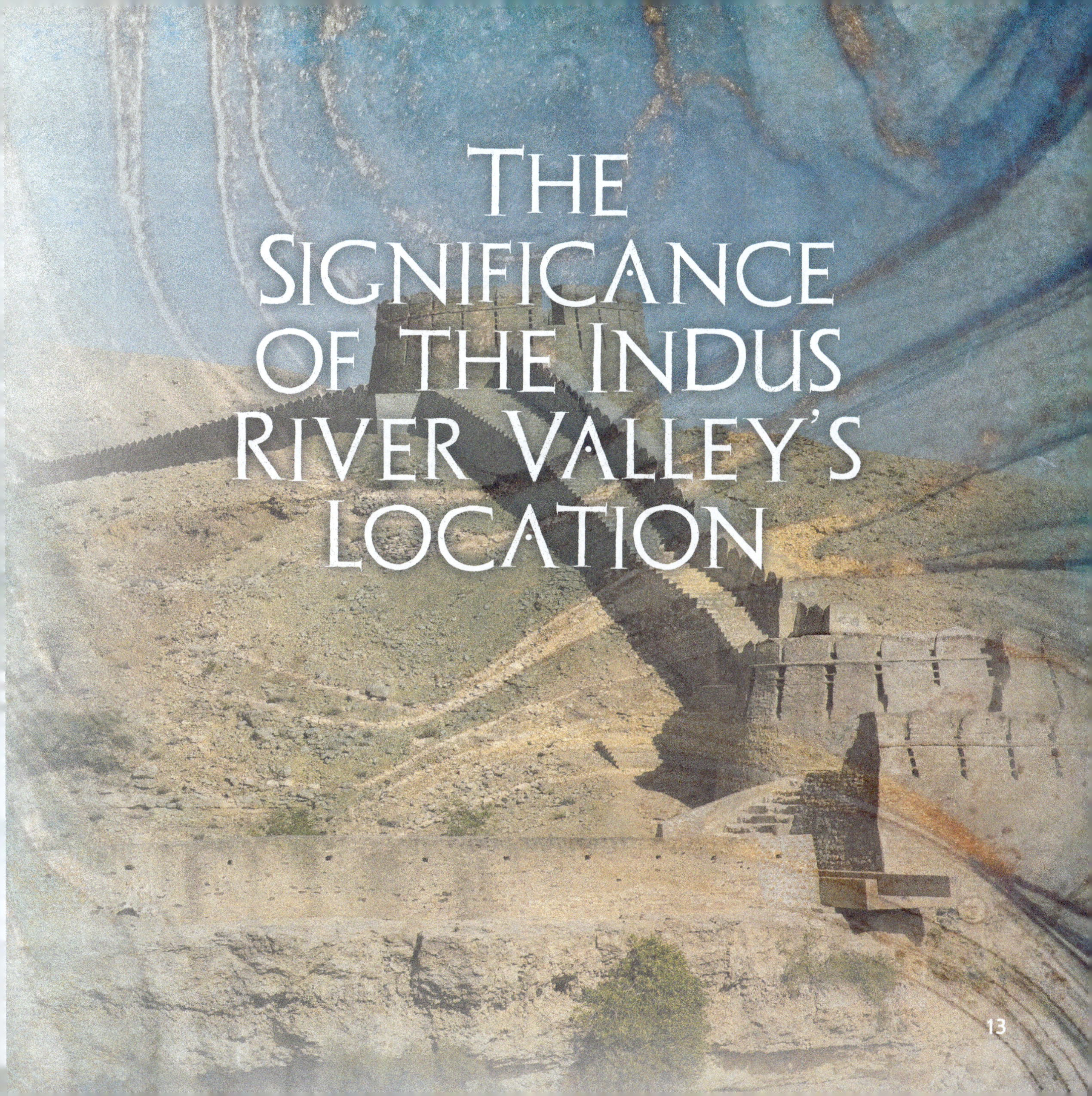

You have learned that there are seven continents on Earth. The Indus River Valley is located on the continent of Asia, but it is found in a unique place. It is on the Indian subcontinent.

The Indus River Valley is located in Asia, on the Indian subcontinent.

High peaks of the Himalayan mountains of Nepal.

The land area that is now India was once a different continent. Through plate tectonics, it drifted into its present location. It collided with the Asian continent with enough force to push up the tall Himalayan mountains.

The Himalayan and the Hindu Kush mountains keep the Indian subcontinent separate from the rest of Asia. The Indus River Valley receives the run-off from the surrounding mountains, ample rainfall, and warm temperatures. It is ideal for agriculture.

Hindu Kush Mountain range

The Rise of the Indus Valley Civilization

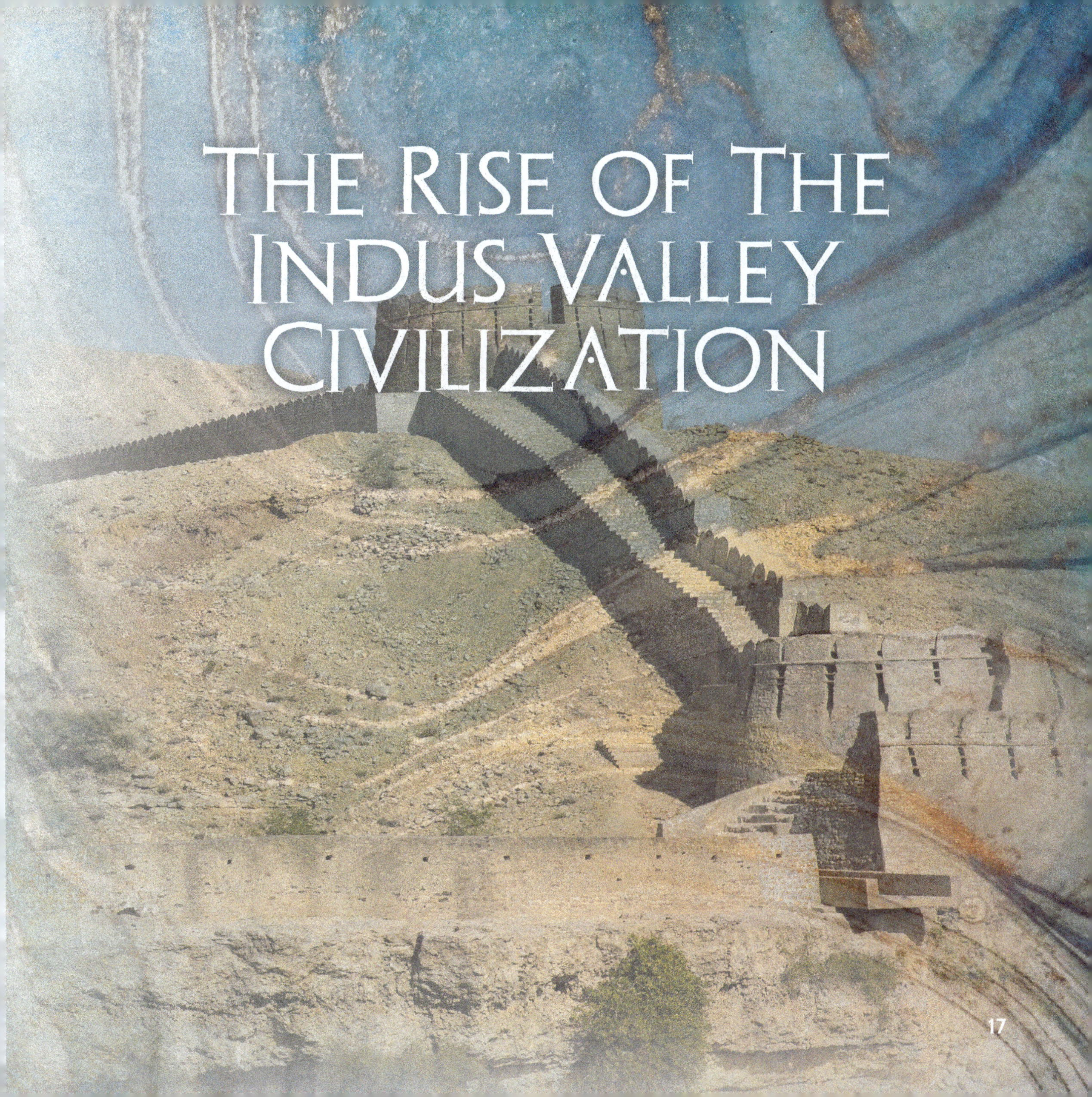

The Indus River was a major reason for the rise of the Indus Valley civilization. The fertile land attracted farmers who grew wheat, barley, and rice. Goats, cows, and pigs thrived in the lush grasslands.

The fertile land attracted farmers who grew wheat, barley, and rice.

The Indus people wove cloth out of cotton, one of the first civilizations in the world to do so.

The Indus people wove cloth out of cotton, one of the first civilizations in the world to do so. There was an abundance of natural resources in the region which allowed the people to build their cities.

From the artifacts that archaeologists have found, we know that the people of the ancient Indus Valley civilization made pottery out of clay, tools out of copper, and jewelry out of gold and silver.

Collection of terracotta Harappa pottery from the Indus Valley Civilization at Mohenjo-Daro, Pakistan.

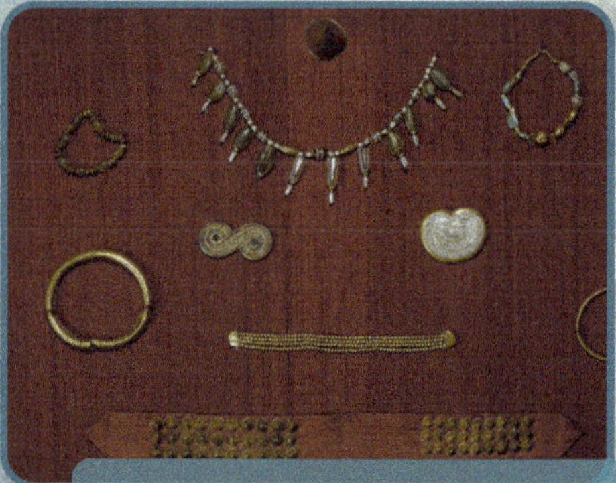

Gold jewellery from the Indus Valley settlement.

Copper implements spear blades from the Indus Valley civilization, National Museum of New Delhi.

The Religious Practices of the Indus Valley People

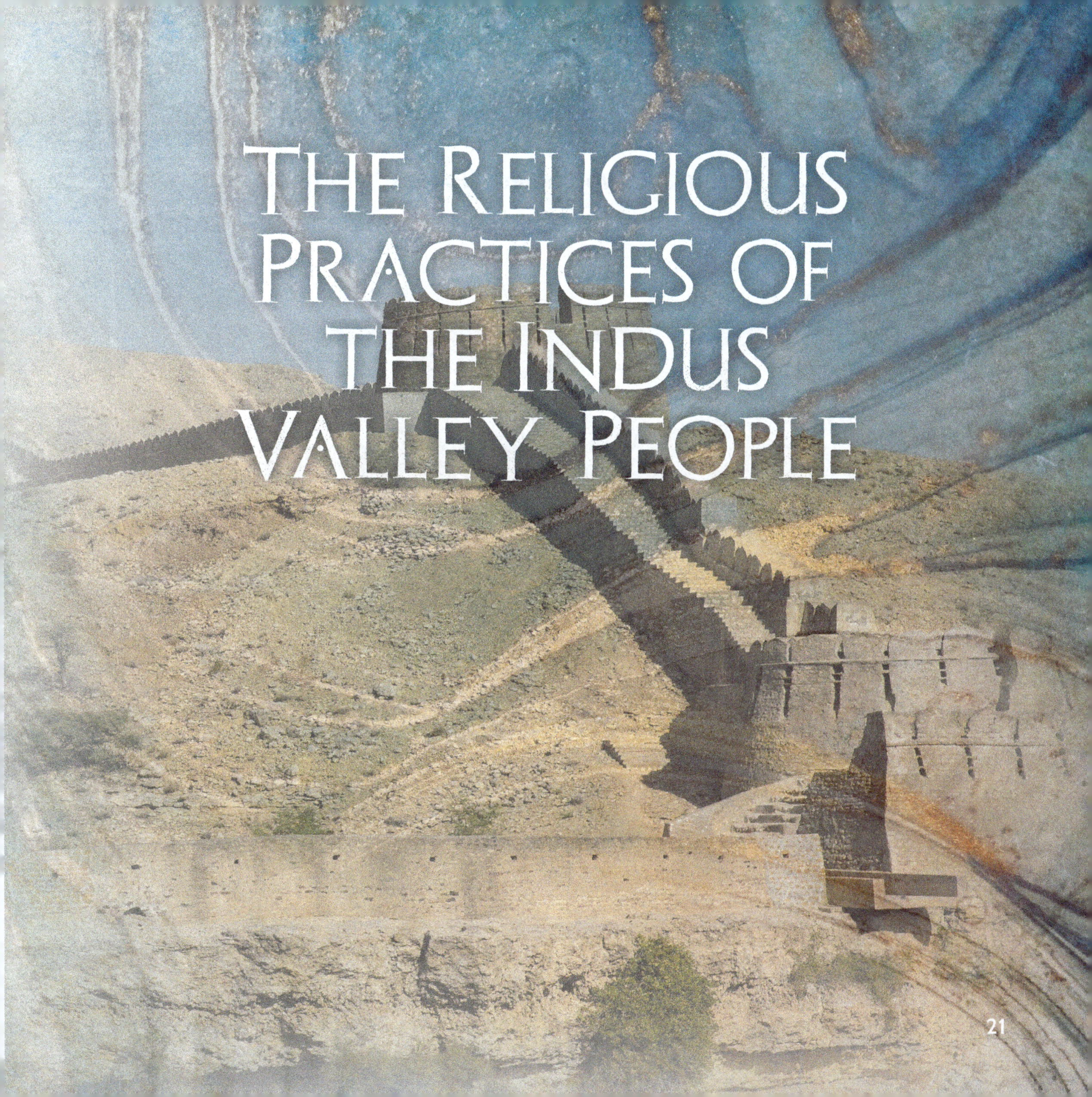

Historians have no way of knowing how the ancient Indus people worshiped. No clearly defined churches, temples, or palaces have been unearthed in Harappa and Mohenjo-daro.

Indus valley Seals from Mohenjo-Daro.

Artifacts unearthed at Mohenjo-daro, Indus Valley, Pakistan.

Display of ancient clay figurines, Indus valley civilization Gallery, National Museum of Pakistan, Karachi, Sindh, Pakistan.

There are no monuments either. Seals, figurines, and relief carvings from the ruins led historians to believe that the ancient Indus people may have worshiped several gods and goddesses.

A different animal, such as a snake or bull, symbolized each deity. Sacred symbols and signs warded off evil spirits, ensured a bountiful harvest, and increased fertility.

Ancient seal of Bull from Mohenjo-daro, Indus valley civilization.

The Ancient Cities of the Indus Valley

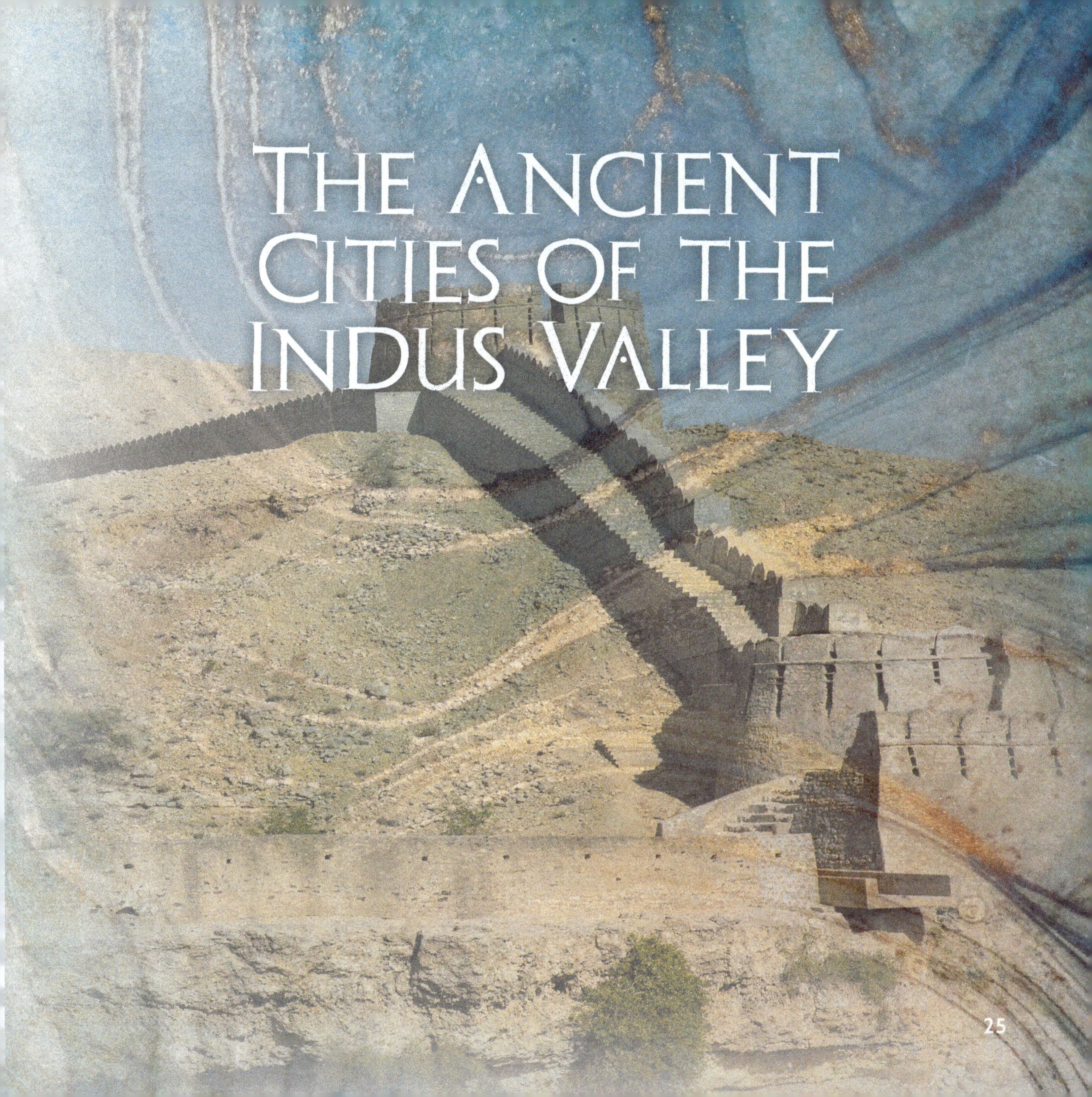

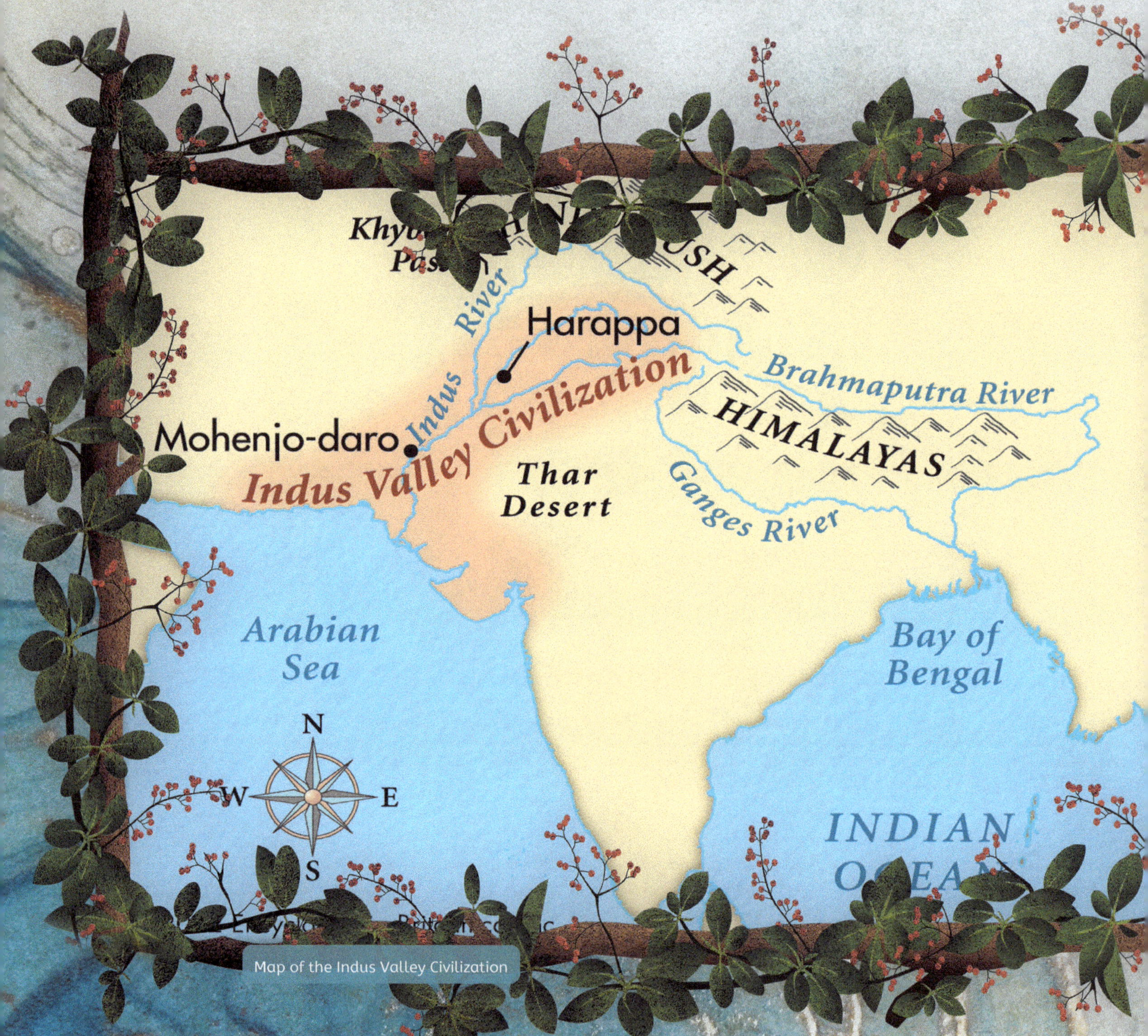

Map of the Indus Valley Civilization

The ancient Indus Valley civilization had two main cities, Harappa and Mohenjo-daro. The details of the cities give researchers insight into how ahead of their time the civilization was. For example, the cities were built on higher areas to protect them from the seasonal river flooding.

Structures constructed in low-lying areas demonstrated their awareness of the flooding. As such, these structures were built on taller platforms.

Houses in the Indus cities

The cities of Harappa and Mohenjo-daro were laid out in grid pattern.

In addition, the cities of Harappa and Mohenjo-daro were laid out in grid pattern. They also had a municipal sewer system. Some buildings were multiple stories tall and had indoor plumbing.

As many as 35,000 people lived in each of the cities. All this was quite advanced for the time period, about 2500 to 1500 BC.

As many as 35,000 people lived in each of the cities.

The Indus River as a Trade Route

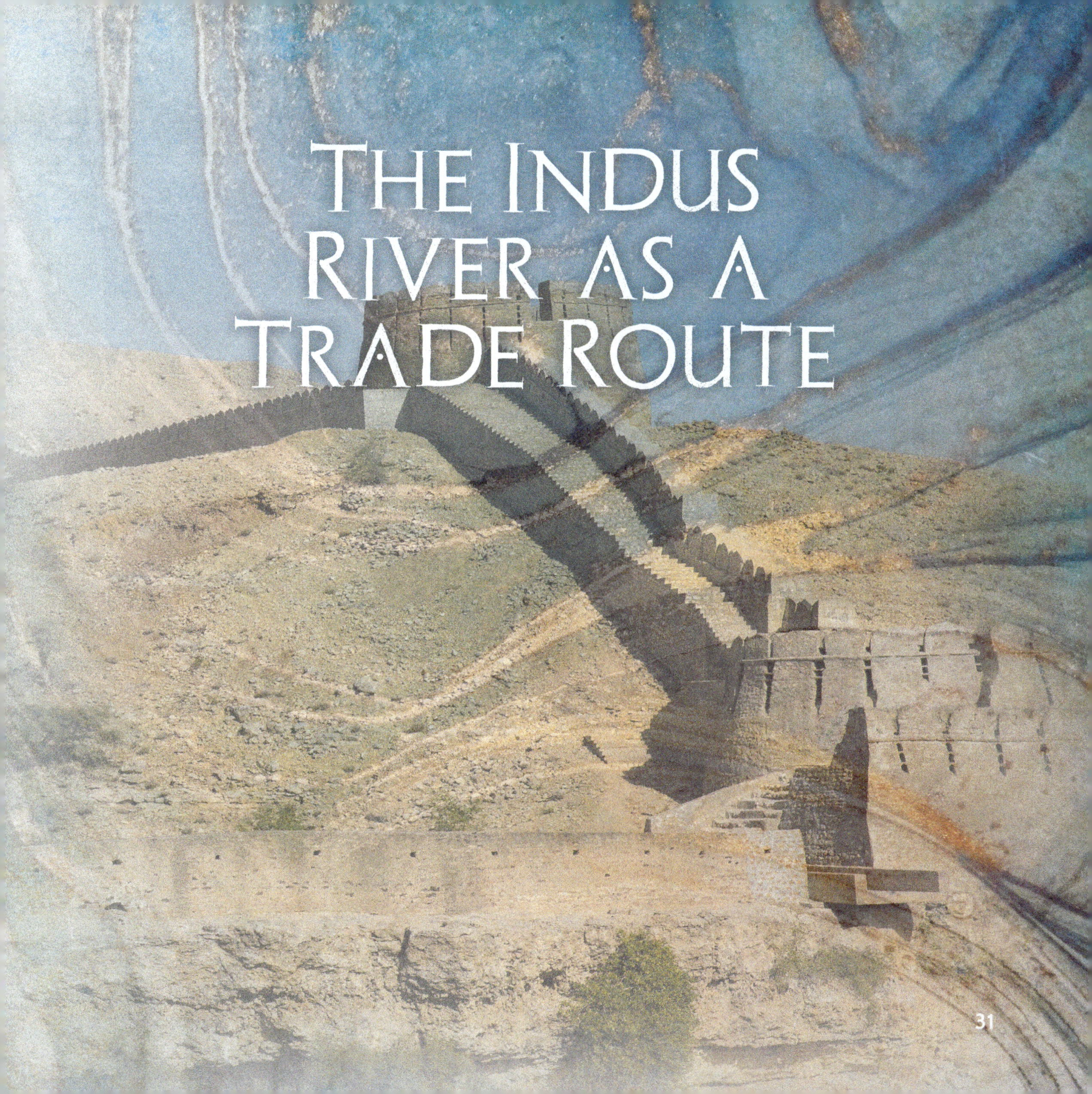

Archaeologists found seals with the images of various animals on them. Other artifacts revealed that the people of the Indus Valley had a written language using pictograms. Although the pictogram language of the Indus Valley people has not been deciphered, the seals that were found are similar to ones discovered in ancient Mesopotamia.

Archaeologists found seals with the images of various animals on them.

Indus Valley-Mesopotamia-Egypt trade routes

This fact, along with evidence located in Mesopotamia, have led scholars to believe that the people of Mesopotamia had established trade with the people of the Indus Valley.

Scholars believe that the people of Mesopotamia had established trade with the people of the Indus Valley.

Moreover, the Indus Valley people likely traded with people living all along the Indus River as the waterway provided a highway of sorts that made travel between areas easier and faster.

The Indus Valley people likely traded with people living all along the Indus River.

The waterway provided a highway of sorts that made travel between areas easier and faster.

A Fairly Recent Discovery

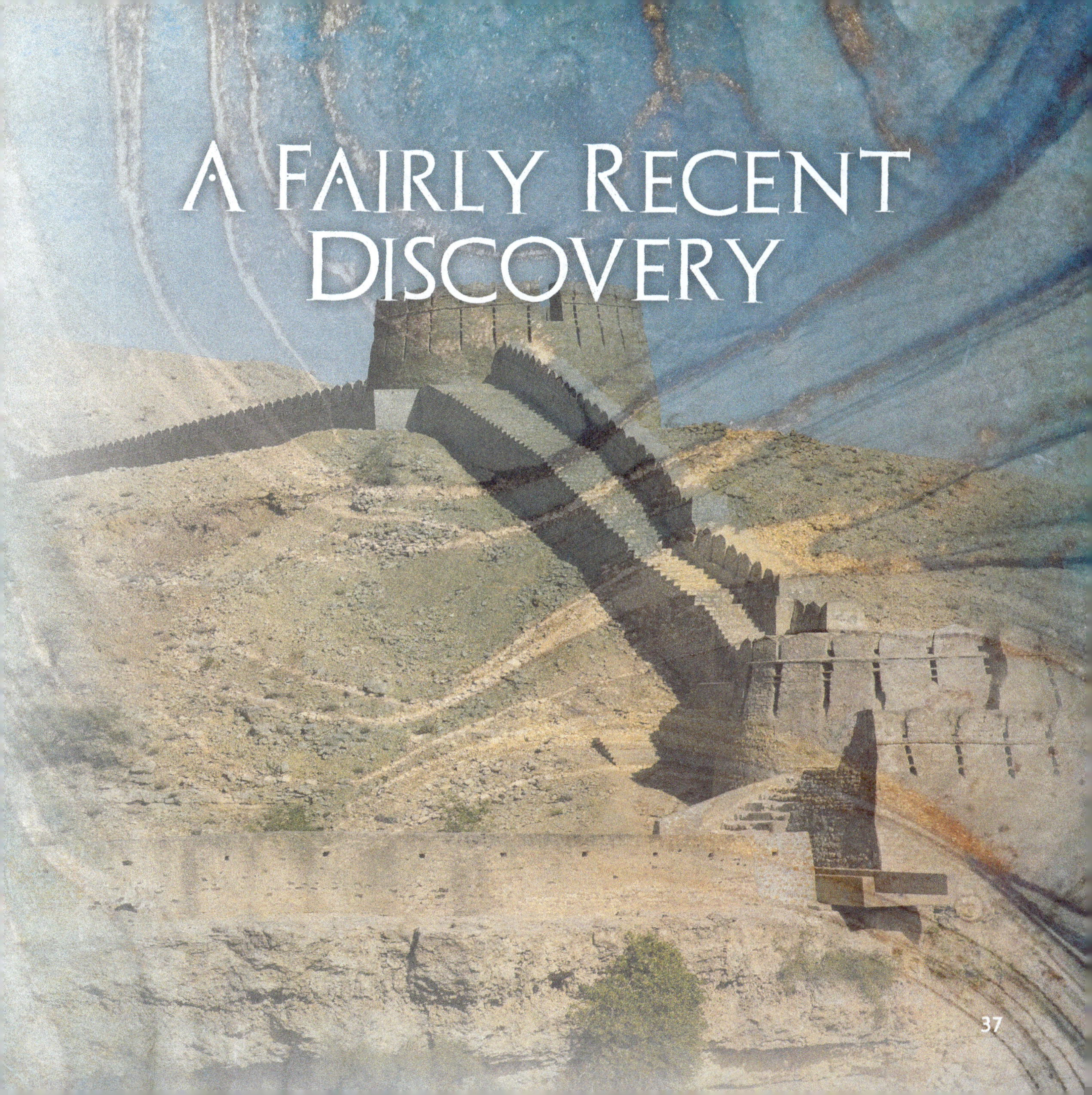

Scholars theorize that the Indus Valley civilization prospered for hundreds of years but began to decline around the year 1900 BC. By 1500 BC, the civilization had completely died out. The once-great cities of Harappa and Mohenjo-daro fell into ruins and were reclaimed by the land. With no written record of its existence, the civilization was nearly forgotten.

Artistic reconstruction of the city of Harappa, in the Indus Valley.

Map of the ancient city of Mojenjo-daro

A panaromic shot of Harappa site.

Mohenjo-daro ruins, Larkana, Pakistan

In the late 1800s, British railroad employees working on construction projects in the area found the remains of ancient structures.

Following the end of World War I, researchers and archaeologists flocked to the region to excavate in earnest. What they found was a previously unknown ancient civilization that was one of the oldest on Earth.

Ruins of Harappan Civilization at the excavation site of Dholavira, Gujarat, India.

Studying the Ruins

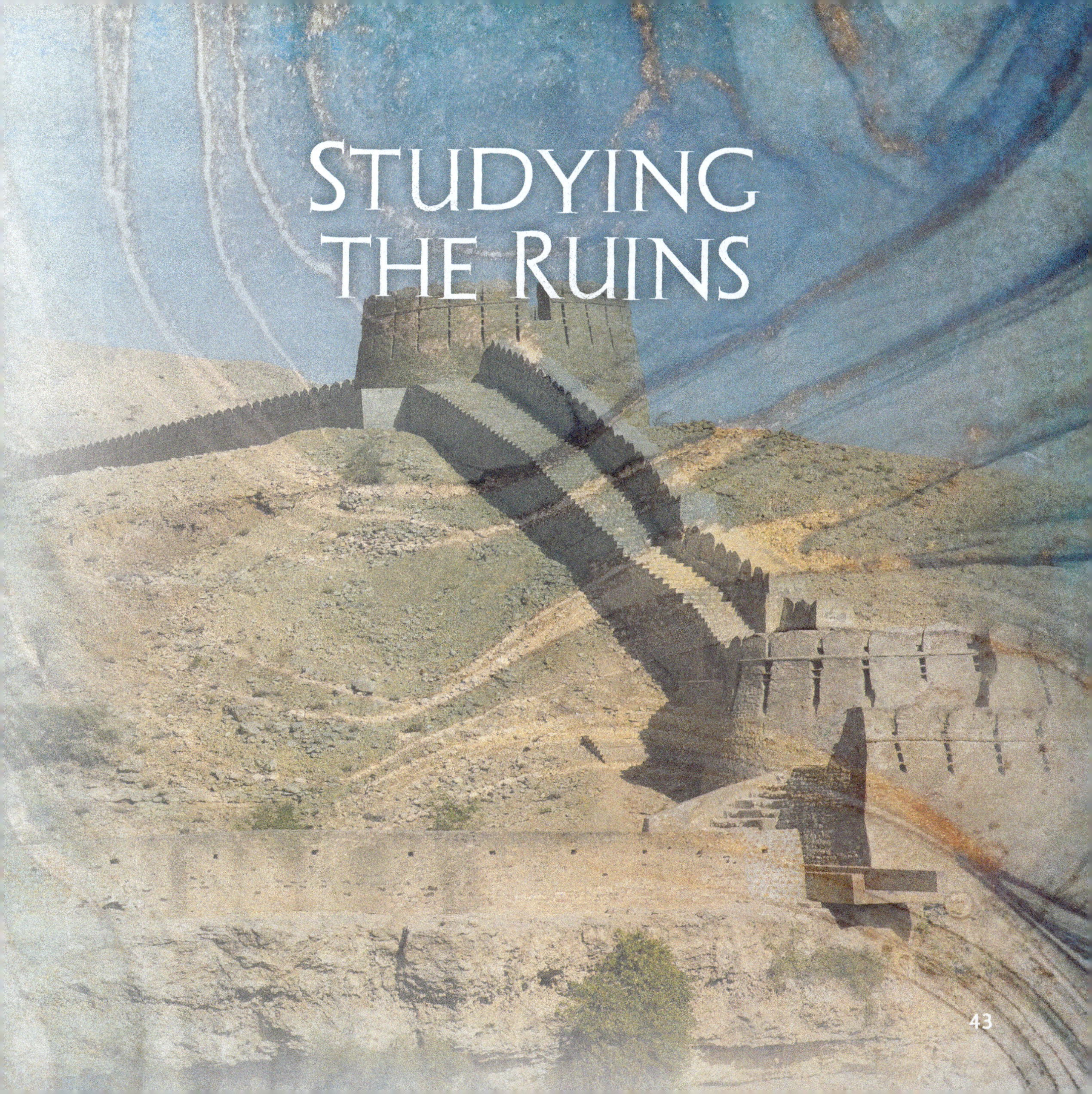

Ruins of Lower Town at Lothal, Indus Valley Civilization.

From the ruins of the cities of the Indus Valley civilization, scholars have been able to glean quite a bit of information about the people who lived there and the type of society they had. Many aspects of the civilization, however, remain shrouded in mystery.

The artifacts that have been found tell us about the day to day lives of the people, but they do not tell us the type of government that they established, their religious practices, or the meaning of their pictograms.

5000 year old skeleton of a human from the Harappan civilization.

Board game, Indus Valley Civilization, Harappa Museum, Pakistan

Terracotta Mask, Mohenjo-daro, Indus valley civilization Gallery, National Museum of Pakistan, Karachi, Sindh, Pakistan.

An antique watch with image of the copper statue from Indus Valley civilization.

Small terracotta jars from the Indus valley.

Perhaps the biggest mystery of all is what happened to the Indus Valley civilization that caused its decline and disappearance. Scholars don't know for sure the answer to these questions, but they have a viable theory. It involves the Aryan people of Eastern Europe.

Scholars have a viable theory for the decline and disappearance of the Indus Valley civilization and it involves the Aryan people of Eastern Europe.

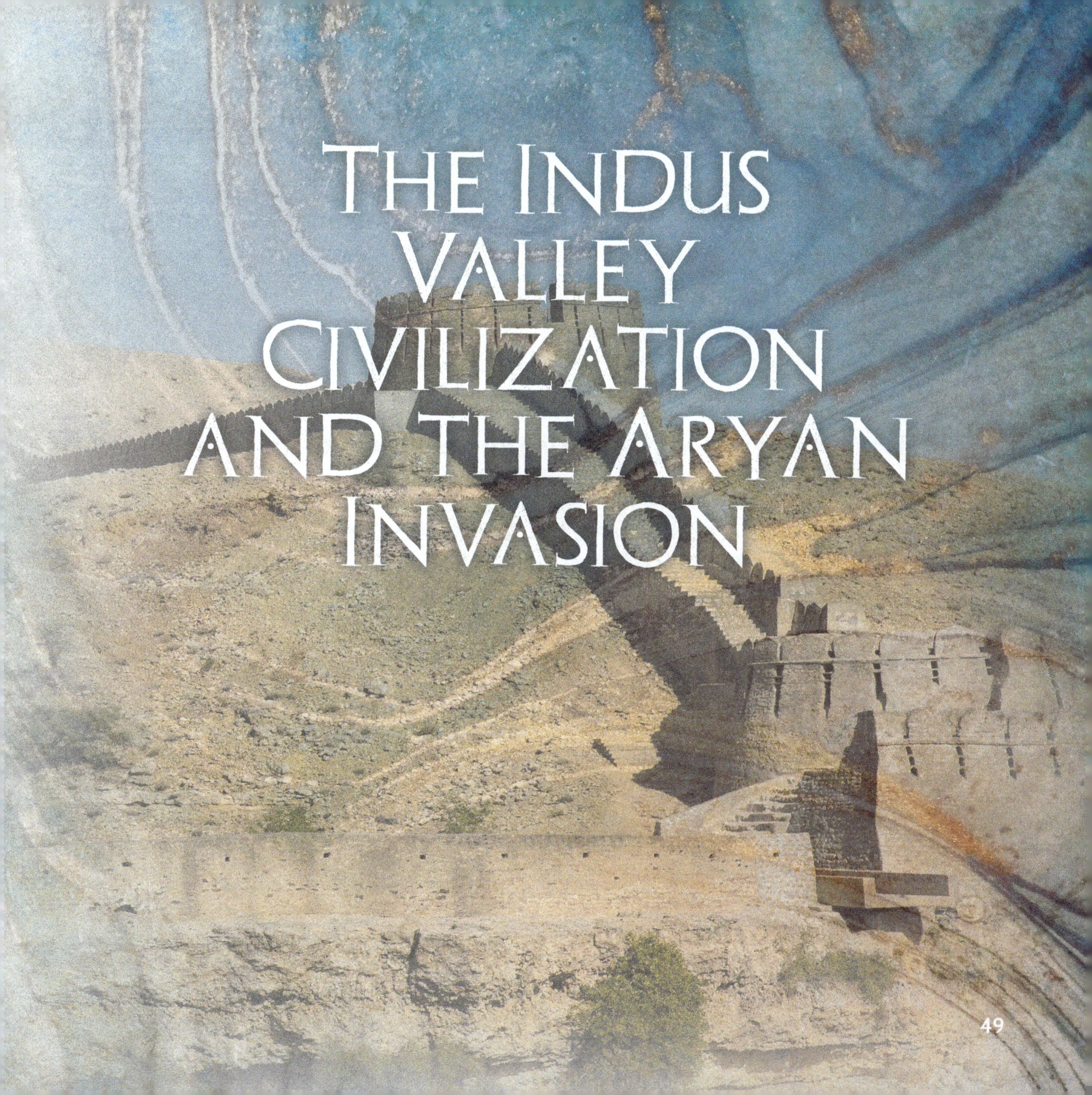

The Indus Valley Civilization and the Aryan Invasion

One prevailing theory explains the fall of the Indus Valley people. It says the Indus people were conquered by Aryan invaders. The Aryan people were fair-skinned, light-haired, tall, and warlike. They came from Eastern Europe. They were a stark contrast to the peace-loving Indus people.

A popular theory suggests that the Indus people were conquered by Aryan invaders.

For much of its existence, the Indus Valley civilization was protected by its geography. The nomadic Aryans crossed the Hindu Kush mountains to enter the Indus River Valley. There is no evidence, however, to support the idea of a large-scale war or mass killing of the Indus Valley people.

The nomadic Aryans crossed the Hindu Kush mountains to enter the Indus River Valley.

Aryan Invasions of India, 1500–250 B.C.
Lines of Aryan penetrations
Consolidation of kingdoms
(PAKISTAN) Modern place name
(AFGHANISTAN)
HINDU KUSH MTS.
Harappa
HIMALAYA MOUNTAINS
CHINA
(PAKISTAN)
Mohenjo-Daro
Indus R.
BAHAWALPUR DESERT
THAR DESERT
Yamuna R.
GANGES PLAIN
Ganges R.
SMALL STATES
MAGADHADA
(BANGLADESH)
Narmada R.
INDIA
Gulf of Khambhat
Mouths of the Ganges
DECCAN PLATEAU
WESTERN GHATS MTS.
EASTERN GHATS MTS.
Tungabhadra R.
Cauvery R.
Arabian Sea
Bay of Bengal
INDIAN OCEAN
(SRI LANKA)
20°N
40°N
80°E
N
250 Miles
500 Kilometers
0

The Aryan invasion has a profound impact on the social order of India, as well as on religion, art, and literature.

We do know that the Aryan invasion has a profound impact on the social order of India, as well as on religion, art, and literature. Could there have been another explanation for the end of the Indus Valley civilization?

THE NATURAL DISASTER THEORY

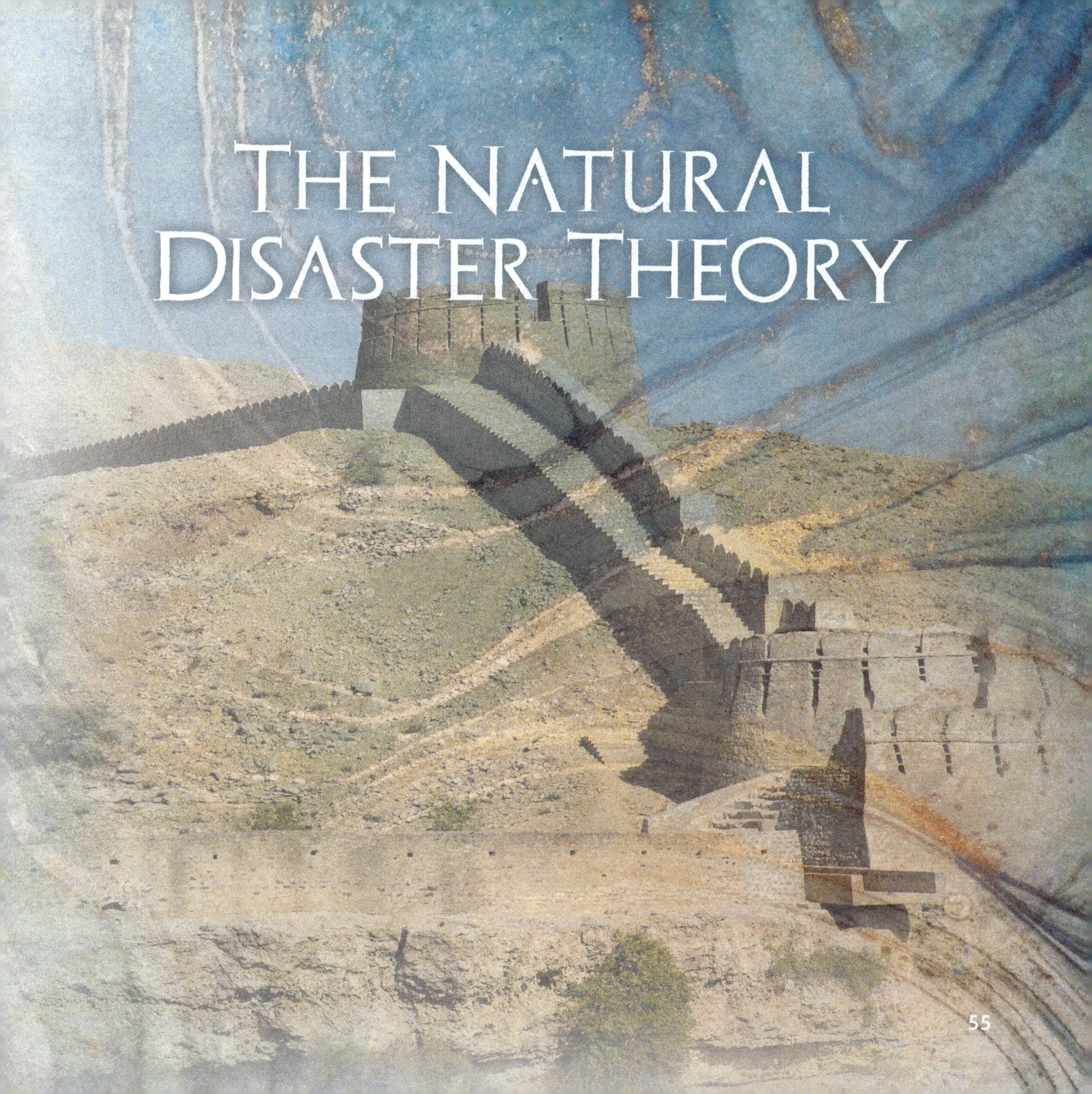

There is another theory that historians developed to explain the end of the Indus Valley civilization. It could be that the region experienced a devastating natural disaster. In addition to seasonal floods, the area is prone to droughts and earthquakes.

In addition to seasonal floods, the area around the Indus River is prone to droughts and earthquakes.

There may have even been a huge flooding event that was much bigger and more destructive than the routine floods.

There may have even been a huge flooding event that was much bigger and more destructive than the routine floods. There was damage to the buildings of Harappa and Mahenjo-daro prior to the Aryan invasion. Attempts were made to repair the damage. They lacked the same sophisticated level of construction that the cities previously enjoyed.

The civilization went into a sharp decline. Perhaps the natural disaster also disrupted agriculture, commerce, and trade. The final straw may have been the arrival of the Aryans who conquered the weakened Indus people.

The final straw may have been the arrival of the Aryans who conquered the weakened Indus people.

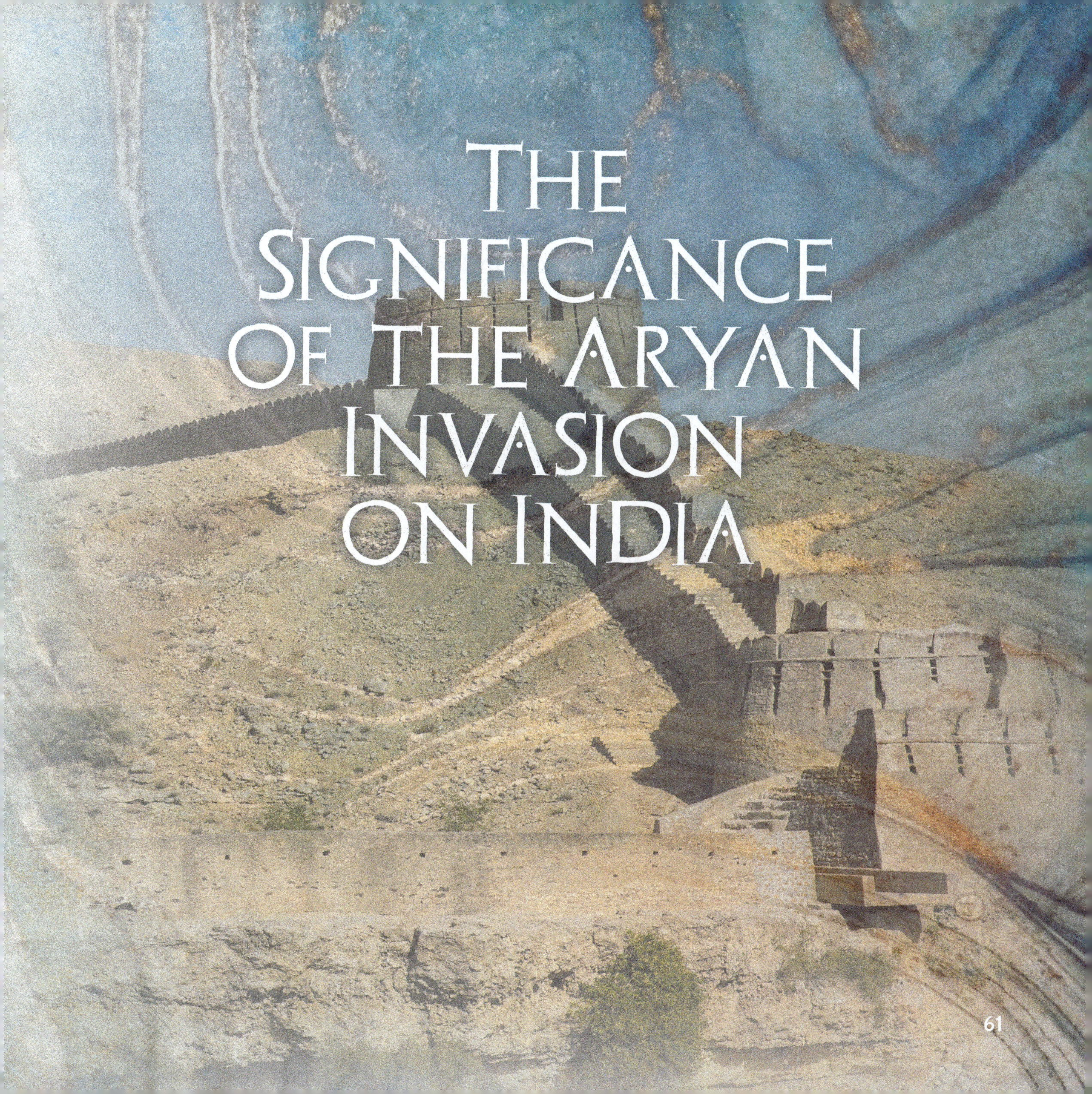

The Significance of the Aryan Invasion on India

The demise of the Indus Valley civilization and the introduction of the Aryan culture had a significant influence on India. The decline of the Indus Valley Civilization left a void that was filled by the Aryans.

The decline of the Indus Valley Civilization left a void that was filled by the Aryans.

In the fertile valley, many of the Aryans became farmers and herders.

By the year 1000 BC, the Aryans were in total control of the region. In the fertile valley, many of them became farmers and herders. They did not become great builders of cities like the Indus people.

Instead, they left their mark on the religious practices and social order of the region. The Aryan religion merged with local beliefs to form the foundation of what would become Hinduism.

Vishnu is the god of Hinduism.

Their religious texts, the Vedas, outline the religious practices, beliefs, and rituals. Veda means "vision and knowledge".

The Holy Vedas

The Aryans also introduced a caste system of social order. Members of society fell into a hierarchy of social classes that they remained in for their entire lives. They could only marry people in that caste and could only work in careers that were permitted by members of the caste. The caste system remains ingrained into Indian society today.

India's Caste System

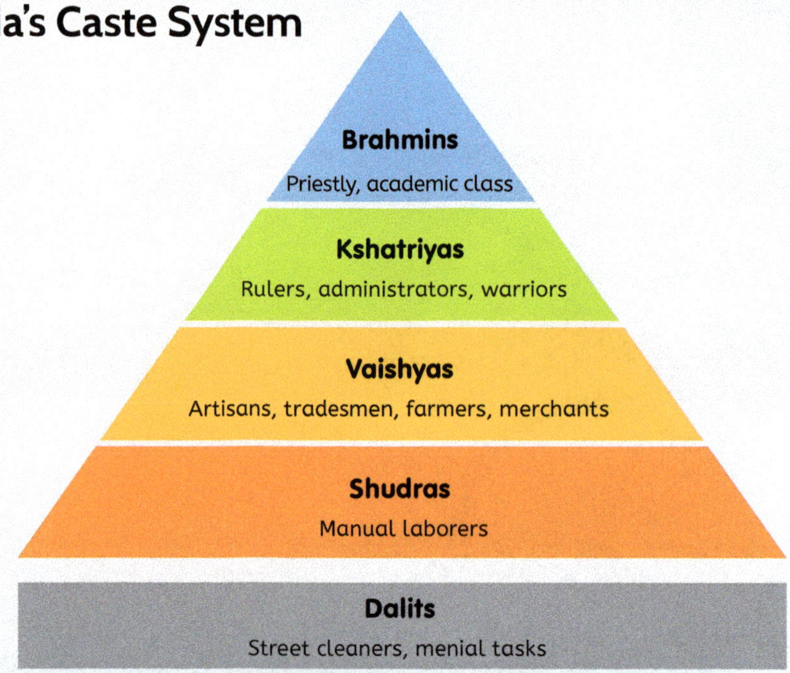

The caste system remains ingrained into Indian society today.

SUMMARY

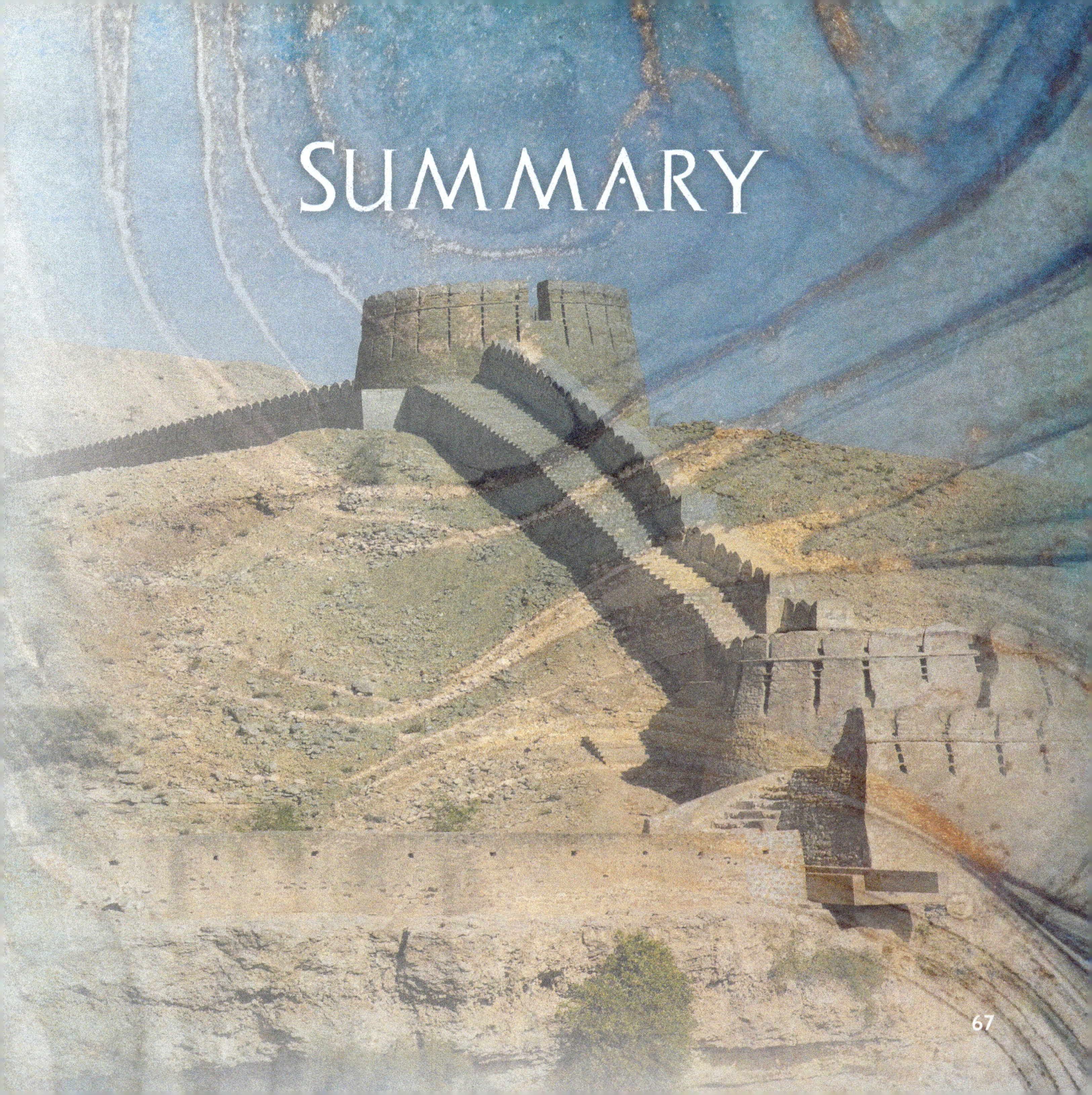

The Indus Valley civilization was one of the earliest civilizations on Earth. It was one of the most recently discovered. The ruins of the once-great cities of the Indus River Valley were only discovered about 150 years ago.

From the artifacts that have been discovered, archaeologists have learned much about the ancient civilization. The Indus River itself, as well as the surrounding geography of the Indian subcontinent, made the Indus River Valley an ideal location for an advanced culture to develop.

Now that you know more about the ancient Indus Valley civilization, you should learn about the other cultures of the ancient world. You may enjoy reading about the Mesopotamian and Egyptian cultures, too.

Ingram Content Group UK Ltd.
Milton Keynes UK
UKHW052140140623
423425UK00003B/158